Praise

AND LONGS FOR OUR...

WORSHIP

Dorry L. Brown

He Lives in Our Praise and Longs for Our Worship

To my daddy,

Waddell Andrew Thomas Sr.

The man who taught me that He is God.

Table of Contents

Foreword

God is Spirit and those who worship Him, must worship in spirit, and in truth. Worship in its purest form, directs its attention and focus on the person of God, His holiness, and glory.

This book is inspirational in depicting praise and worship as the highest calling of God. God is worthy to receive glory, honor, and power, for He created all things by His will. Acknowledgement of the worthiness of God will increase consciousness of His person and presence.

He Lives in Our Praise and Longs for Our Worship is a must read for those who are tired of empty religious rituals and desire spiritual intimacy with the Father. Receiving this teaching will stimulate an enlightening experience, that will forever alter our approach to the way we seek Him.

The Lord has anointed Pastor Dorry to bring this revelation of biblical truth to the body of Christ through this book. And I believe that all who read it, and receive the revelation, will be restored, and gain new insight of God's will.

Pastor Joe L. Poe

Mt. Zion Missionary Baptist Church

Snow Hill, 2019

When I think about my childhood
and young adulthood, I can clearly
remember my church experience. The first
thing that comes to mind is the Good
News Club. Every Tuesday, the missionary
in my neighborhood gathered all the local
kids and taught us Bible stories. She used
character cut outs and moved them back
and forth across a felt board, then gave us
snacks before it was time to go. During
snack time, she always asked if there was
anyone who wanted to accept Jesus. And

after every lesson I stood up smiling, and openly welcomed Jesus into my heart. Without even knowing it, I was making a commitment to God, and to myself, that I would receive His love and walk in His likeness. As I got older, I sought the mentorship of seasoned leaders, to help guide my studies and build my relationship with Christ. Before I knew it, I could recite His word, and quote Scripture with my eyes closed. But it was not until much later, where I would really delve into my church experience.

Music was a big part of my upbringing. I can still hear the drums and the tambourine, but I liked the songs the most. There were tons of hymns, but when the deacons started with *"At the Cross"*, *"Blessed Assurance"*, or *"I'll Fly Away"*, the entire church joined in without hesitation.

After the songs came the devotional period. Each person would begin their testimony by saying *"First Giving Honor to God, to the Pastor, Saints, and Friends, I would like to thank the Lord for how He kept me over the dangerous Highways and Byways..."*. After this everyone would sing:

> *"I have decided to make Jesus my choice.*
> *You know the road is rough and the going gets tough.*
> *And the hills are hard to climb*

I started out a long time ago,

And there is no doubt in my mind

I have decided to make Jesus my

choice".

People stood up all over the church
to share their story, then once about five
people shared, the Pastor would introduce
his sermon. This was the routine of the
Baptist church where I was raised. As I
visited and mingled with other churches, I
noticed they used a similar system, and
did so for many years.

In the recent years however, the
church has done away with the devotional
period, and has implemented a praise and
worship interlude. During this time the

praise and worship leader guides the praise and worship team into songs that are usually fast and up-tempo for the praise break, and slow and relaxed for the worship session.

No one has ever explained to me why this change took place, or how it came to be. But now I realize, that this change was made to encourage the believer's relationship with God. After coming to this realization, I was inspired to learn more about praise and worship. And in the knowledge I obtained, this book was born.

What is Praise?

"Let everything that hath breath praise the Lord.

Praise ye the Lord" (Psalm 150:6).

The speakers of our local assemblies commonly reference the theme of the testament above, perhaps so often that we have become disconnected with its significance. To obtain a new grasp of this seemingly elementary text, we must first recognize its august subject: praise.

Praise is most frequently defined as: to acclaim, applaud, or celebrate; to glorify and honor. Sources may complicate the meaning of the word through convoluted synonyms and behaviors. Nevertheless, praise is simply expressing admiration of, paying tribute to, or complimenting someone, whether it be for a specific action or deed fulfilled. Furthermore, praise can be executed by anyone, for anyone, or in any approach, given that the needed incentive is present. You can praise the doorman at a hotel for his friendliness, or the cashier at Walmart for her patience as you count your quarters, or even the school janitor for tolerating the messiness of the children at your child's elementary school. Unlike worship, however, praise is not dependent upon a relationship, as it can be offered absent a deep familiarity with, or closeness to a person, or even to God Himself. Praise is offered based on a specific, individualistic interaction, encounter or experience.

As such, Scripture declares and affirms that *all* living creatures are capable of speaking highly of the Lord, complimenting Him for His work, and expressing admiration of Him and His exaltedness. We immediately consider people as the primary proponents of praise, but plants, animals, and the smallest of microorganisms also house the capacity. There are no prerequisites for extending praise, as the skill is deeply embedded within us all, regardless of age, profession, gender, spiritual status, or economic class. Varying backgrounds may produce different experiences of and with God, but when we think of His Goodness, as it manifests itself in any given situation, we can all praise Him, and it is only just and right for us to do so.

Therefore, even if you do not know God, or understand the power of who He is in all His glory, you can still praise Him, and He still deserves that praise, because you still see His handywork, and reap the benefits of His labor. Praise is a small gesture that conveys thankfulness, and in it there is a rushing power, one that produces an intense peacefulness and that creates the availability for demands to be fulfilled.

Praise can be done by opening our mouths, dancing with our feet, clapping our hands, crying in His presence, or any combination of these expressions. The Bible discusses and acknowledges several types of praise, given that it is so remarkably elaborate and personal. I encourage you to routinely implement at least one of these approaches, in order to optimize your spiritual experience, and stimulate an increase in God's recognition, of your appreciation.

There are different meanings in different styles of praise. If you commonly exhibit praise in the *Barak* form, where you bow or kneel in respect, then embracing the application of praise in the *Tehillah* fashion by singing melodies unto the Lord will verbally and melodically demonstrate your love. Modifying your technique from the *Shabach* form to conform more to the *Towdah* method, shifts one's emphasis and expression from verbal commandants of affirmation, to a more clearly visible display of God's richness. Perhaps, if you routinely praise in a quiet tone, it would be of great value to attempt to *Shabach* by raising your voice for all to hear how good He has been to you. Employing diverse forms and systems of praise reveals to God your true heart and the sincerity in your appreciation of the work He has done for you.

Bearing in mind that God embodies multiple roles and performs the corresponding duties of these roles with Divine, unbounded and endless love, one will naturally conclude that He deserves our praise, and that it is indeed well warranted. If God remains God in the midst of our sin and disobedience, we can surely rejoice in His righteousness and ascribe to Him who He is.

Reminders

2 Corinthians 2:14 (The Amplified Version)

- He always leads us into victory.

"But thanks be to God, who always leads us in triumph in Christ, and through us spreads and makes evident everywhere the sweet fragrance of the knowledge of Him."

Psalm 77:14:

- He performs miracles.

"Thou art the God that doest wonders: thou hast declared thy strength among the people."

Nehemiah 9:6 (The Amplified Version)

- He is the Creator.

"You are the Lord, You alone; You have made the heavens, the heaven of heavens with all their host (the heavenly bodies), the earth and everything that is on it, the seas and everything that is in them. You give life to all of them, and the heavenly host is bowing down [in worship] to You."

Psalm 68:19

- Bears our burdens.

"Blessed be the Lord, who daily loadeth us with benefits, even the God of our salvation. Selah."

Chapter

2

What Happens When You Praise?

"Enter into His gates with thanksgiving, and into His courts with praise: be thankful unto Him and bless His name" (Psalm 100:4).

To reinforce the subject of the previous section, we must know and take to heart that God is worthy to be praised, and that He is dependable and always on time.

Despite our choices, His character never changes. He shows up in each of our situations, steadfast and unmovable. Whether you are a new convert battling the temptation to backslide, a Sunday service-skipping single parent, or a teen dabbling in street life, God is holding you in His hands. He does not exercise favoritism in the execution of His favor and mercy, and in this operation, He is well and most deserving of our praise.

Take note that our praise is not a *requirement* to inflate God's ego; rather, it is a symbolic acknowledgement of our reverence for Him, and an indication of our longing for His presence.

Sincere, honest praise has the power to incite change, and possesses the ability to shift any atmosphere. Therefore, and now that we have examined and defined praise, let us explore three objectives our praise can accomplish.

1. Deliver

Acts 16:16-26 briefly outlines an event amid Paul's and Silas's journey. Upon entering a neighborhood town, they are greeted by the market psychic girl, who mockingly yells and boasts of their Godly work. Disgusted with her immodesty, Paul commands the spirit out of her, and the girl is no longer possessed.

In the girl's freedom, her owners grew angry because their business weakened and perished. They became bitter and beat Paul and Silas, then dragged them into the market square, where the town guards arrested them. At the open trial, the townspeople furiously shouted as the guards roared their charges. A public beating of Paul and Silas was ordered, and after the mauling they were jailed under maximum security.

While incarcerated, Paul and Silas began to pray. They prayed and sang, sang and prayed, and worshipped. The other prisoners became overwhelmed with astonishment, but the two did not stop or reduce their efforts. Suddenly and unexpectedly, an earthquake erupted, completely dismantling the jailhouse. The doors flew open, swinging off their hinges, and Paul and Silas were free.

There are two examples of deliverance in this section; one is spiritual and the other is physical. Prior to arriving in the Macedonian village, Paul and Silas were actively engaging in praise and worship, as this town was only a stop along their quest to spread the gospel. They had been on a mission of seeking new leaders, to expand their ministry, as the congregation steadily became "stronger in faith and larger in size." (Acts 16:5)

Thereafter, and because of Paul's spiritual acuity, he was able to take control over the demonic influence that was governing the marketplace psychic and set her free. She endured spiritual deliverance because she was freed from the force that was tormenting her.

Conversely, Paul and Silas experienced physical deliverance. Their prayer, praise, and song pervaded the entire ambiance of the prison, thus initiating a shift in their existing state. Their prayer and song were a cry out for help from God, and He responded by rousing the earthquake that prompted their escape. In the face of their troubles, they sang and praised; in their acuteness they were able to administer deliverance, and in their faith, God delivered them.

Singing and praising can offer deliverance from any source of affliction or imprisonment. In doing so, you are acknowledging your lack of control over your position, and this immediately invites God to intervene.

2. *Summon His Presence*

In life, we frequently experience a vast
array of challenges that become
increasingly demanding and strenuous
over time. We commonly respond by
venting to family, friends, coworkers, or
for that matter anyone that will listen, all
in a quest to obtain some sort of relief
from the mounting pressure.
Unfortunately, we quickly grow
dissatisfied and frustrated, as these
measures do not yield the results or sense
of alleviation for which we long.

We are not, however, compelled to
experience this cycle of weariness, for if we
learn to acknowledge and summon God

during adversity, we can rapidly transition out of and move beyond its frustrations and limitations. Praising God is a way for us to communicate with Him and to summon His company. Praise is the medium that transports us out of our current dilemma and into a renewed sense of conviction. Praise is the channel, the gateway, and the link that unites the Earthly realm with the Heavenly realm.

When you surrender your plight to God by giving Him the praise He duly deserves, you are joining your earthly troubles with the harmony of Heaven, thus permitting yourself to function in the temperament of Jesus, and bring peace to your contest. In this connection, we are able to see as He sees and walk how He walks. From this juncture, it is rather elementary to then step beyond our strife. Henceforth, our praise gets His attention, summons Him to our situation, aligns the two realms, and allows God to manifest in a way that grants us the power to rectify and realign our discord under His authority.

3. Build our Faith

At the point of conversion, we accept Jesus as our personal Lord and Savior, and establish a covenant with God, declaring that we agree to walk by the dictates of the Holy Spirit, while Christ assures that He will stand with us, accompanying us on our path. In this covenant, both parties have agreed to tread life's hardships together, even though during times of drought and affray this proves to be difficult for the believer, as the covenant is commonly overlooked or forgotten. Rather than surrendering to the pressure, however, we must attempt to solve our problems independently, and to react to these challenges by praising God. When we dutifully operate in this way, our faith is revitalized and the covenant is revived. Our praise embodies our faith in Him, and allows us to be reminded of the promises, gifts, and rewards that He has bestowed upon us.

Reminders

Just Praise

Psalm 34:1

"I will bless the Lord at all times: his praise shall continually be in my mouth."

Psalm 145:3

"Great is the Lord, and greatly to be praised; and His greatness is unsearchable."

Psalm 56:4

"In God I will praise his word, in God I have put my trust; I will not fear what flesh can do unto me."

Acts 16:25-26

"And at midnight Paul and Silas prayed, and sang praises unto God: and the prisoners heard them.

And suddenly there was a great earthquake, so that the foundations of the prison were shaken: and immediately all the doors were opened, and every one's bands were loosed."

Chapter

3

Am I a True Worshiper?

"But the hour cometh, and now is, when the true worshippers shall worship the Father in spirit and in truth: for the Father seeketh such to worship Him. God is a Spirit: and they that worship Him must worship Him in spirit and in truth." (John 4:23-24).

Let's begin by defining the word *worship*. Worship is defined herein as the act of acknowledging God for who He is, all that He possesses, and all that He will eternally be.

The foundation of this teaching on worship is derived from the scriptural passage cited at the start of this chapter. Henceforth, it is imperative that we wholeheartedly grasp the message being conveyed.

The passage opens with the word *but*, which completely refutes any prior thought or statement. Similarly, it is highly anticipated that this enlightenment will nullify the believer's former understanding of worship, while introducing a fresh and more rewarding perspective.

In today's church setting, worship has become associated with song, music, and a sequence of behaviors. We frequently enter into worship when the musicians heed the lead of the praise and worship leader. The tempo slows and a palpable pulling back on the drums is felt, followed by the praise and worship leader singing a gentle, relaxed song with simple lyrics. As a result, the congregation begins to cry out, closes their eyes, and lifts their hands, occasionally swaying with the rhythm of the medley. If a member or visitor arrives late, they will immediately know which phase of service they have breached based on the knowledge and awareness of its steps and stages. This is the general worship setting of most churches. In examining the congregation, we may even see children engaging in worship by singing along or raising their hands, then celebrating them for being in tune with the Spirit. This system and these behaviors, however, do not even begin to epitomize the essence of worship or what it entails. As a people, we have conditioned ourselves to worship in this composition; the music is the stimulus, and we promptly react externally, hence we now associate worship with calmness and certain, known behavioral responses.

Nevertheless, *this* is not worship. Our worship has developed into a Sunday morning service ordeal, as we have become driven by, and accustomed to, the feeling and impression of the church experience. Instead, there should be an opportunity to focus and center on the intimacy of God, giving ourselves over to the experience of allowing our being to be saturated with His splendor.

Worship is an inward experience, one that is based on a fervent relationship with God. Additionally, worship is a lifestyle, and cannot be masked, assuaged, or represented by a Sunday sway. Furthermore, God recognizes the true worshiper. That person and his genuine connection to God is headlined and emphasized within the scripture. In this highlight, it is specified that the true worshiper is being sought after.

Consequently, this means that everyone that is worshiping is not necessarily a true worshiper, and that not every method of worship is truthful or sincere. God is actively seeking true worshipers, because not all worship and all worshipers are operating under His truth; hence, not all worship is received.

A true worshiper is one that worships God in their spirit, and in the truth that has been revealed to and deposited within them by the Holy Spirit. To be classified and acknowledged as such, we must take time to develop and cultivate our relationship with God. To do so, we must routinely study His word, commune with Him, and seek Him. There are several benefits of being a true worshiper, and we see that when we learn to worship in truth, the quality of our life is enhanced, and we obtain immediate results from God.

Reminders

Psalm 29:1

"Give unto the Lord, O ye mighty, give unto the Lord glory and strength. Give unto the Lord the glory due unto his name; worship the Lord in the beauty of holiness."

2 Kings 17:38-39

"And the covenant that I have made with you ye shall not forget; neither shall ye fear other gods. But the Lord your God ye shall fear; and he shall deliver you out of the hand of all your enemies."

Psalm 100:2

"Serve the Lord with gladness: come before his presence with singing."

Exodus 23:25

"And ye shall serve the Lord your God, and he shall bless thy bread, and thy water; and I will take sickness away from the midst of thee."

John 4:24

"God is a Spirit: and they that worship him must worship him in spirit and in truth."

Psalm 63:1

"O God, thou art my God; early will I seek thee: my soul thirsteth for thee, my flesh longeth for thee in a dry and thirsty land, where no water is."

Chapter 4

He Lives in Our Praise

And Longs for Our Worship

"From the rising of the sun to its setting

The name of the Lord is to be praised [with awe-

inspired reverence]" (Psalm 113:3).

For so long, I have sat before the
Lord so that I may clearly hear His voice
and thoroughly articulate His will. It has

been my goal in these pages to share with
the reader a fresh perspective on the
elements of praise and worship. Praise
and worship are not activities that we
haphazardly engage in during a Sunday
service. Praise is our most effective
method of honoring Him. There is no term
or phrase within the language of man that
fittingly illustrates His greatness. With
respect to worship, our worship of God will
never supersede our knowledge of Him.
The true worshiper does not need to be
told when to worship, nor instructed on
how to worship, because worship is a
lifestyle that has no off-switch. We seek
out opportunities to praise because we are
grateful for something He has done, but

we seldom take the time to get to know Him or understand who He is through our worship. When we do take the time, however, to know and sincerely appreciate Him, we incite an overflow of His blessings and grace.

I believe the principles I have presented can enrich the spiritual experience of all who read these words, and the points below will be extremely useful in taking full advantage of the content learned throughout this book.

1. He Lives in Our Praise

The basis of our praise is to declare or express our love of God. Furthermore, praise welcomes Him to occupy our space and dwell in our presence. When we praise, God lounges in His chair, and completely absorbs the way we magnify and glorify Him. He does not need our praise to obtain contentment, nor is it a requirement for Him to do His work. Nonetheless, He is comfortable and delights in it, because He welcomes and feels our acknowledgement of His worthiness and excellence.

2. The Power of Praise

In that our praise can impose deliverance, build our faith, and beckon the presence of God from His heavenly kingdom unto our Earthly arena, it is clear to say that praise is a glorious instrument that carries a powerful influence. We must realize, however, that this is no ordinary, everyday power.

The New Testament frequently uses the Greek word *Dunamis* to describe various entities and events. Here the term is interpreted as a mind-blowing, Earth-shattering, marvelous power. Isn't it marvelous how the walls of the jail shattered to free Paul and Silas? Isn't it marvelous how the walls of Jericho came tumbling down at the sound of the trumpets? Our connection to God enables us to break through barriers of fear, doubt, and disbelief, because the power of our praise welcomes the presence of our God.

3. Worship requires Relationship

Contrary to popular belief, our worship is not governed or evaluated by the antics we display. We can do all the movements and still not enter into worship, because worship cannot be choreographed. Instead, worship is founded on the framework of a sound relationship with God. This relationship is carefully cultivated, and based on the worth we ascribe to God, because we worship Him in accordance with how worthy we deem Him to be (Psalm 29:2).

When we are capable of receiving and harvesting God's deposits in our spirit, and returning these revelations back to their ultimate Source, we have evolved into true worshipers. To further comprehend the impact of, and the immediate rewards associated with, true worship, we must examine the events surrounding King Jehoshaphat (2 Chronicles 20), Hannah (1 Samuel 1), and King Solomon (1 Kings 3).

A Token to Always

Remember...

Praise ushers us into His dwelling, and worship is how we bathe in His glory when we get there. And once we learn to properly engage in praise and worship, we will find ourselves in a never-ending parade of victory.

The content within the Daily Keepsakes portion has been provided by two of my dearest friends, Elder Sandra Brown and Pastor Tim Smith.

Fear Not

"For God has not given us a spirit of fear, but of power and of love and of a sound mind." (2 Timothy 1:7)

What do you do when the rubber meets the road and it's time to walk through your fear? Do you retreat and let fear have its way? Do you cry or pray? If faced with fear, walk through it with your head held high, knowing that God is on your side!

-Elder Sandra Brown

Take Heart

"Be of good courage, and he shall strengthen your heart, all ye that hope in the Lord." (Psalm 31:24)

In life, we endure many different situations at various times, and we can easily become overwhelmed. Yet there is joy in knowing, that the Lord will strengthen us. He is our refuge, and our resting place; He is our present help in our time of trouble. So, hold your head up, don't give up, and remember the joy of the Lord, is our strength.

-Elder Sandra Brown

A Godly Mindset

"Set your affection on things above, not on things on the earth. For ye are dead, and your life is hid with Christ in God." (Colossians 3:2-3)

Sometimes we have to take a spiritual trip, so that we can prepare ourselves to hear the Spirit of God. To do this, we must reposition ourselves, and set our affection on things above. We have to remind ourselves that our life is hidden in Christ in God, and because of this, we can walk in the assurance that all things have already been worked out for our good.

-Elder Sandra Brown

He Cares

"Casting all your care upon Him; for He careth for you." (1 Peter 5:7)

There is no need to worry, nor to be anxious, for worry will slow you down. When Jesus died on the cross, He took care of everything; all our problems, and any situation we may face. He loves us, so in whatever you are going through, cast your care upon Him.

-Pastor Tim Smith

Pray

"Pray without ceasing." (1 Thessalonians 5:17)

Never stop praying. No matter how hard it gets, prayer will see you through your tough times; it's your compass, your light, your lifeline. Prayer is your key to success, so don't stop praying.

-Pastor Tim Smith

The Plan of God

"For I know the thoughts that I think toward you, saith the Lord, thoughts of peace, and not of evil, to give you an expected end." (Jerimiah 29:11)

God's plan is much more desirable and foolproof than any plan we can draft. His plan has long term, everlasting benefits, designed to give us results that we could never imagine. He's willing to make our head spin in amazement and power. I urge you to follow the plan of God and not your own, because you will have a far better turn out in the end.

-Pastor Tim Smith

Trust God

"Trust in the Lord with all thine heart; and lean not unto thine own understanding. In all thy ways acknowledge him, and he shall direct thy paths." (Proverbs 3:5-6)

Sometimes we feel like we can do things all on our own. But when we do, things don't always go as planned. To keep from making unnecessary mistakes, we must acknowledge God in all our ways. God keeps us from dangers seen and unseen, so trust in Him, rely on Him, because through His guidance, you will never go in the wrong direction.

-Pastor Tim Smith